*Where Is North*

# The Gerald Cable Book Award Series

# Where Is North

*Alison Jarvis*

Silverfish Review Press
Eugene, Oregon

Copyright © 2017 by Silverfish Review Press

Cover art: *Our Woods* © 2002 watercolor and ink by Lorin Bernsohn

English translations © 1985, 1997, 2002 by Roger Greenwald

Rodger Moody was the 2015 GCBA final judge.

Published by
Silverfish Review Press
PO Box 3541
Eugene, OR 97403
www.silverfishreviewpress.com

Distributed by
Small Press Distribution
800-869-7553
spd@spdbooks.org
www.spdbooks.org


Library of Congress Cataloging-in-Publication Data

Names: Jarvis, Alison, author.
Title: Where is north / by Alison Jarvis.
Description: First edition. | Eugene, Oregon : Silverfish Review Press, [2017]
Identifiers: LCCN 2016047719| ISBN 9781878851680 (pbk. : alk. paper) |
      ISBN 1878851683 (pbk.)
Classification: LCC PS3610.A78 A6 2017 | DDC 811/.6--dc23
LC record available at https://lccn.loc.gov/2016047719

9 8 7 6 5 4 3 2 First Printing
Printed in the United States of America

# Contents

IV

I AM STANDING BREATHLESS

V

LISTEN

In Memory of Larry
and for Lucas and Amanda

Where do we find now
a way to connect what is scattered.
The trail in the stars, the compass needle's course
or the lines in girls' hands
that are like the wind through the roses.
For it is late

soon the river will carry off my images;
hillsides, reflections of houses, a beloved face—
it will carry them out to sea.

        *Slowly— —*
        Rolf Jacobsen

                *Translated from the Norwegian*
                *by Roger Greenwald*

# Where Is North

# I

## THE SAME HOUR HAS COME INSIDE MY BODY

# The Same Hour Has Come Inside My Body

Here in Venice there are houses newly ochered
and some, once green are gone
to celadon. White light at noon
dazzles off stone; latticed and fretted
like handkerchiefs, white houses float
in surrender over the canal.
Even the palazzos of Venetian red—
color of clay, color of old blood,
wave in light off water. Everything moves
and nothing
              really begins or ends
in Venice, where color is memory
of color; umber, siennas—burnt and raw, the earth
of other places. Always as we near
each arched stone bridge that enters
the canal, there is that moment before
we apprehend the memory of the bridge
on the body of water. How much
fullness depends on surrender
and disappearance. The gondolas—
their black lacquer slipping through
darkening waters—look like coffins
and they look like cradles.

I used to believe in the orderly
progression of time, the slow shift of tenses.
Now month after slipping month,
the future falls back on itself. Damage
to your body. Disorder
in regions of your brain where each day
more neurons shut down. Once you told me
you pictured them like lights clicking off
one by one, in some alien town
where everybody goes to sleep at night.

                    Only in Venice
do you sleep all night. All night it seems
I watch you and I hear
bells in the campaniles ring, each
sound suspended through darkness
until it begins again.

And here, behind pine green shutters
in the slatted afternoons—
light splitting into ribs against the dark—
we can make love again,
not as a diminished act, but containing,
like a photograph. Or like a mosaic,
the way the Byzantines created them,
using just enough mortar for a single day;
placing the astonishing shards of colored glass
at angles that would refract the light
a hundred ways.

# At the Diebenkorn Show Without You

*#11—oil on canvas*

Is this California? It could be
anywhere, the way the overpass
straddles the street near its vanishing point.
That blur of green not so much grass
or trees, as words I rush through

to get to the heart of the story.
Where I grew up near the prairie, empty roads—
wind-flat, abandoned—
curved so far off, I'd tell myself:
Beyond *that, that*

I'm here now. The nascent red daub
in the distance still draws me. You'd say:
Look at the foreground,
how just a quick vertical
paints in the present.

Remember the cabin
we rented one summer, set back
at a turn in the road? I kept overshooting—
When you find yourself passing the pond, you'd say
you've gone too far.

Turn around. Come back.

# The Bach Suites

If I'm careful of tubes and wires, maybe I can find a way
to fit my body next to yours
in the high, narrow bed. If I can unplug the alarm
that warns of falling, no one will know
we are lying together listening
to quartets. I would hold your hand.
The man on the other side of the curtain
won't wake. He never does,
not even at laughter I can't stifle when I read
Tom Sawyer, the only book you ask me for—
Tom, the master of escape, free finally
on that island in the river, for a time.
I could use the margin of time
between Mr. White, the aide, undressing you, lifting you
into bed, and the night nurse, Ramon
bringing the last medication that tomorrow
will allow your right hand to move a little.
I'm glad it's the hand you used to bow, which I see here
as 'bow,' as in bending from the waist,
as a man to a woman in a courtly gesture.
You always had something of the old world
your father left behind in Vienna. But now,
I mean to bow a cello.
We could listen to Schumann or Beethoven—
so much music I would have loved to learn about
from you, but never did. I don't know
if it was because you couldn't offer
or I couldn't ask. I thought you should know
how much I wanted that. I could lie with you
listening in the dark, but not to the Bach Suites
that set your fingers moving each morning,
your door closed by 8, your sound
through every room.

# Time after Time

Only yesterday in the garden
of the hospital, out of nowhere I started humming
this tune and you, who I have never in my life
heard comment on a popular song, said, *That's so beautiful*—
clearly, and for the first time in months, loud enough
to be heard. *Who wrote it?* And I, who have always loved
this song, didn't know.

# Daylight Savings

Because he's ill and can't, I change
the clocks, forgetting the faceted crystal
with silver hands beside his bed. So when he tells me
I'll be late, I know better. I always know
better now and say so. As though
he's already gone, as though it's really possible
to change the clocks.

# Ask Me

### 1

You were not the kind of man to take
coffee to your wife in bed every morning,
but if I asked, you would and it pleased me.
I didn't do it often and I always thanked you
in a formal way like the kind of man you were.
One day before I realized I had stopped asking,
you said, *I wish I could bring you coffee*—
Still each morning you managed to make it,
leaning on counters for balance,
kitchen quiet except for the whistle
you need to cue yourself: *Now move: One foot
in front of the other: this is the way
you do it*. You tear open the bag
with your teeth.

2

I'd start writing you a message—*J. called.*
*Don't meet him 'til 4 o'clock. He has to take L.*
*to the doctor. He was up all night with—*
The notepad always too small, I'd give up,
write, *Ask me*, then *Love*. I needed to give
the whole story. As though without each detail
you'd never understand my meaning. And now
when you may never speak again,
I sit by your bed talking for hours
as though you asked me
to explain everything.

# Three

        Last night fitting your body
into its lift, the nurse asked me
    if three was my lucky number—

        she was looking at three
bridges I'd lined up in front of the clock
    when you kept asking

        for your cello, and three
incised ivory tiles—river, cloud,
    mountains—upended

        in front of the bridges.
At home they centered
    one of the domestic altars

        I was always building without
knowing. You called it
    the altar of the foyer table, the one

        in front of your painting of me
with our daughter in my arms. You gave her
    eyebrows like wings.

        *Three*—I wouldn't say lucky,
but I've always loved
    things in threes. I even had

        three places. Those pillar
candles on the sill—ghosts now
    the light's leached out their color—

        were grass-green, purple, blood
orange the day I brought them home
    from the studio I wrote in.

I had to give it up because of money
and the cold. I should have known I couldn't hold
a pencil, a thought

to its end in a skylit space
in winter. A bird got trapped there
over a weekend. It didn't die

was only dazed, but I thought
about a Lakota winter count, a pictograph
I saw as a child, cold so intense

crows froze in the air
and dropped dead near the lodges. Nothing
could have protected me.

Not the heaters circling me
like wagons. Not the painter with offers
of scotch, coffee, his body.

What if I could have held on
to that room? What if I could have
held on

to the office in the village—
the couch, the patients,
the white noise in the waiting room

keeping their stories
a secret. If I died drowning you said,
someone else's life

would flash
before my eyes. With you so sick
I gave up

that place too, so now
I'm down to one.
Do you see me here

in this room above the river
where I've lived
    half my life?

    Do you hear
the white-throated sparrows
    that winter in the park whistling

    the song, you
with your musician's ear,
    could always give back

    perfectly? Listen!
*Tseet, Tseet*—
    it's the call they use

    when they fall
out of view, one
    from the other.

# From a High Place

When I open the book
I'm reading you, your mark falls out
and floats in the light
to my bare knee. Another summer—
I've started counting now—three,
since your mind finally locked
itself up with your body. Your mark
is a sketch done in ink, a man falling
backwards through the white space
of hotel message paper. The Graff Zeppelin,
Stuttgart. *What year I wonder?*
You were still holding on
to perspective.

# A Dream, Soon After

We were on a crowded bus
going to a play. I found a seat
near the front, but you

had to stand farther back.
I glanced out the window
and there you were in front of a diner!

I called you without a cell phone
and you answered without a cell phone.

"I had to get off before you," you said.
I didn't even ask why. Nothing

in my mind
but my ticket in your pocket.

# II

## SKY, RIVER

# Where Is North

We used to lie there
Backs flat in snow
Fifteen below at noon, the glare
Blinding us. All those contests—
Who could last longer—
Arms, legs, furiously shaping
Angels around us.
You pulled a mitten up
With your teeth and cold
Ate away the tongue touching
Your metal bracelet.
It went on forever, that white
Field behind the house. Broken
By barbed wire, stitches
In the snow.

Tonight across the courtyard
I heard a drunk screaming.
I could barely keep myself
From bolting, the way we did
Nights our father blazed
Like struck, dry pine. Then
We'd break—no stopping, no
Coats or shoes. Who could
Run faster. Who could run
Farther. The vast field,
The stitches, the endless white.

# Ice Fishing, Lac Qui Parle

At night light shines in the houses
on ice. Our fathers silently
hunch over mouths of dark water,
wait for silver fish to flash
in the black just below them.
In the blackness surrounding, the sky
lets go of its snow. I think of the houses
as lanterns, or words
that rise in the throat.

Weeks ago, when they were certain
the lake had frozen
beyond melting, they
hauled their houses onto the ice,
dragging them like lives
they longed to inhabit. How far

away from them we wait
in lit kitchens. Listen,
there are words that simmer in us
like liquid, almost soundless. Soup on the stove,
steam rising to the slanted ceiling. Lost
drops gather there and fall
to stream the frigid windows.

At night the wind is fierce
enough to bend the rigid pines
and drown the sounds of dark
longing, the hunger that pulls
weaving bodies to the surface,
mouths open, shaken fins
flinging drops of water,
silver in the fire.

# Skaters

We belonged to snow and ice,
to Dodd's Pond at Christmas, released
from classes, shining our way
through the morning dark,
like miners. We'd skate out
together, alone, to astonish ourselves;
past lunch, past supper
past any possibility
our numbed fingers could ever
untie our laces.

# Itasca

We drive a road laid straight
to cleave the cornfields. Dust
from husks, split stalks,
shuts our eyes like smoke.
Six of us crushed
in the old black car, my sisters
and I so close in back
our arms and legs almost lock.
My father's long bones
fill the driver's seat.
The baby's between them,
so my mother has to crook
an elbow out the window
and it's burning.
In the rear view I can see
my father won't stop
for food or rest. We're fleeing—
When we reach the river
far north, we'll leap
from the car, run
into the water
to be baptized, all of us,
our stunned bodies
longing to be saved.

# When I Think of My Mother Laughing

it is already dark, already late in the year. My mother,
my sisters and I are in the small living room
with the over-sized fireplace and the over-size fire.
My father is already drunk at the American Legion bar.
It is always just after supper
and we are always pretending.

My mother is in her place—
the swivel chair next to the fire, and tonight
I am a school teacher from South Dakota finally possessed
of enough courage to run away with my corn farmer lover.
Stick-straight hair scragged into a bun, new glasses
at the end of my nose, I deliver a monologue of passion
in my best prairie accent. My mother laughs so hard
the swivel tilts. The small panes of a window divide up
the night, each of us reflected in her own square of darkness.
One cone-covered bulb from the lamp in the corner
pools light around me. And I think I am the happiest
I will ever be.

My sisters are sitting on the couch sinking
into laughter, deep cushions of sky-
blue chintz, cabbage roses blooming
around them. The room is beginning to turn
as I twirl with my lover across the thinning green
carpet. And in the mullioned bay window my body breaks
into many bodies. I am a long line of girls
whose red skirts swirl like wind
circling the house. Rising on laughter,
above the room, above the house, finally
I am far enough away to see nightbirds
below me against the snow—not flying
but poised on the wires, so at home
in the dark.

# Each of Us Diving

The old dream. Yesterday we drove
up and down and over your Ohio
for hours, looping it
like rope around us, as though
a river could keep things
from falling away. But the rising
water in my dreams is always
the Mississippi, and we are always
children. Even now
nights I lie in the dark and wait for sleep,
sing the old hymns mother sang,
*until my raptured soul shall find*
*peace beyond the river.*

There was a storybook we read
about a town the river took. I see
a cow and the peaked roof
of a sweet house bobbing, the heads
of children just above the water.
Were they saved? I wish
I could tell you, but I only remember
each of us diving
for the father too drunk to save himself,
and the mother so tired of rescue
she quoted John of Revelations,
*His voice is the voice of rushing waters.*

We both still live on rivers,
and though there are days like yesterday,
when light off the water builds
its own sweet shell of peace;
I think of us like the parents of lost children
you read about, the ones
who can't give up their old lives,
who sit waiting
thirty, sometimes forty years.

# My Father's Songs

Finally the earth was warm enough to plant
his grave. Hard frost took us in October
so we forced the nursery bulbs—hyacinth, crocus

chionodoxa they call *glory of the snow*—in light
wells outside basement windows. Then we buried them,
pointy tips through the soil, around his marker. We were all digging

the shallow holes and someone started singing *Ramona*. I think
it was my older sister. We broke into parts then
for harmony on *Annie Laurie*, and *Lulu*, he used to sing

for mother. Jake, the littlest was down on his knees,
cupped mouth, shouting into holes *Pa,*
*Pa, can you hear us?* My father used to tell the story

of Will, his friend, who when he married Emma
bought a plot there. They'd picnic Sundays, spreading
a cloth over their land, sitting on their grassy graves.

Jake and I lay down on the grass. Clouds,
dimpled white as the oldest tombstones, were moving
so fast we could barely name their shapes.

# Another Life

My mother, my aunts, their voices
drifting through porch screens
like fragrance, told stories
with endings like covers
of books thudding shut.
*But that was in another life*
they'd say, and I
would try to picture that life
that was really a series of lives:
separate but coupled
like cars on a train,
the first disappearing
just as the next turns the curve.

It's May again,
and I'm sitting alone
across from the esplanade gardens,
babies in strollers, mothers
bending over them
whispering,    dogwood
falling like paper.

# Leaving

Sometimes I'm still standing
at the back of the train,
lost track my only perspective—
poles, splintered, crossed
twice at the top, receding,
I can grieve everything—
river, wheat, my mother waving
her white handkerchief, initialing
the spring.

# Sky, River

This morning, early, you call out
*Sky Alert!* the old imperative
we use to signal each other—
*Leave Everything!* and run
to watch the sun burn down
the Hudson, throw fire on water,
melt sky carmine to magenta like a Rothko.
These are the rules—
No one calls out unless they can imagine
nothing more beautiful, and no one, ever
doesn't come. How many times
did the sky rescue us? Now the river

is the Rhine. The children gone. Barely standing
you hold on to the evidence
of river and sky, call out *Fog*—
thick, the color of tallow, milk, zinc.
Then there's a dark line of river just below
and the fog is a shade
on the window of the room. You can almost
reach out and lift it.

# III
# DAKOTA

# Dakota

How can it be—the smell of my grandfather's barn
On the 5 AM wind of a Bahamian Island? Faint, ancient
Wood disintegrating into dust, not rot, like the felled
Banyan behind the borrowed house here.
Sweated leather saddles hung from tangy spikes. Rust,
The mix of hay and urine. *Oh*—the smell's cayenne—
And in my memory, not the air. Last night's home-concocted
Antidote for a sore throat that left me speechless. Cayenne,
With honey in hot water, no hint of the burn,
The forty minutes it takes to swallow
What's in the cup. And now here's my grandfather,
Not in the barn, but later, in the small parlor of a house
He bought after the farm was sold
For schools, playing fields, a pool. Places for the young
To begin their purposeful suburban lives.

He is always in the corner, outside the circle, outside of speech,
So far into his own silence he's more
A part of the field he leans into, small blue and white flowers
That could be borage and pea blossoms, as though
My grandmother chose the plastic upholstery to cushion
What was lost—long rows of vegetables, the self-
Sufficiency my father was so proud of. *During the depression*
*We grew everything we needed. All we bought was salt.*
But I know my German grandmother, practical daughter
Of the brickworks, what drew her was the plastic. Pretty,
But a surface you could wipe clean of any stain. I am watching
My grandfather, shock of white hair, cigarette thin as his fingers,
Striped shirt so crisp there's still the iron's hiss on it. Never a syllable.
Though at this moment I imagine him
Saying my name, a voice opaque as his eyes and dry
As barn dust or prairie grass. Who told me

The story of disappearance—scrapheap wagon, oxen, the tall grass
In waves that left no trace of a family? Whose ghost

43

Held shut the sod hut's door against the implacable?
Snow buried everything, whole herds of cattle,
An aunt, a brother. I knew a man who went searching
For his ancestors' homestead. Hillside dugout, sod squares
Cut from the treeless prairie—it had melted away like snow,
Back into the earth. If I could revise the story, if I could
Make my family prosper, pour the honeyed prairie light of late spring
Afternoons into their empty winter bodies, make them candles
For their windowless rooms; if I could give them a river through
Bluestem, Wild Rye, Indian Grass, sound beyond killing winds—
Summer—meadowlark and mockingbird,
Could I give them speech?

What words were left, what breath, in the dead
Defeat of the way back? When I think of that return, that punishing
Sky, oppressive, not one vertical
To challenge it, I like to think of my grandfather later,
In an old photo, "1915" written on the back. He's a lineman
For the telephone, a job he's got to save up
For the farm. Who took this picture out here
In the country? Not another soul, or house
Or tree, so it's hard to tell how tall the pole is.
His long frame my only reference, I'd guess
Sixty feet at least. The ten pin cross arms look like steps
He's climbed. His right hand's raised to claim
The sky. Perching birds, the instrument of song deep in each
Feathered body, will gather on these wires that lead the eye
To the edge of the picture. It's still winter,
No hint of thaw, the Mississippi rising, the floods that drown
Acres of corn somewhere in the future. Then we will hear
The earth gasp, the roots of plants dying
For air, pore space filled with water.

Right now my grandfather looks happy.
He doesn't smile, but he holds his cap in his left hand
As though in deference to this moment:
The sound he knows is humming
Through the air around him. There is so little demarcation

Between his white hair and the vast background
Of winter sky that despite the heavy jacket, the steel-
Shanked lineman boots, he seems weightless, his face
The resolve of a chord that, hearing, we could be lifted
Into perfect understanding, into the simplicity
Of the picture: black and white, the snow,
The poles, the wires in parallel lines neatly
Dividing the sky.

In a plane, I close my eyes until there is no possibility
I might glimpse flat patterns of farmland laid out
Below me: Houses, barns, outbuildings lost
To mere speck and shadow. My grandfather's deep set eyes
When I open mine, look back at me from the window.
I see his bones in my face, locate his absence
In an old confusion: Why only untethered do I feel safe?
There are those who can't enter the hatch without tapping
The side of the plane with their knuckles. The farther I get
From everything, the more at home I am. Snow does that too—

Enough of it takes you away from everything
By taking everything away. When my father died on the day before
        All Souls,
Ten feet of snow had already erased the backyard of my childhood
        and swallowed
Every sound. Yesterday my friend said: *History's a novel. Who's telling*
*The story? When? Why?* I think it was the last Christmas we had on
        the farm.
I think when my grandfather set the tree ablaze with what seemed
Like a hundred tallow candles, what he wanted was the sound, the
        long draw
Of our breath, its release into awe.
And we were told a miracle
Could occur at midnight. If we didn't venture out, risk exposure,
Get too close to the barn by crossing the snow—a white sheet
Of wordless paper between us—the animals would speak.

# IV

## I AM STANDING BREATHLESS

# 75 Marshall Avenue

I'm the grinning baby waving
the flag, and wearing a hat
like Uncle Sam's. The men in our family stand
staggered, in their uniforms
home from Europe or Japan.

The camera loves them.
It catches light that bounces
off brass and lavishes fabric
with the glow of vestment.
Or maybe it's the light itself that loves,
protective, heightening the shine
of medals and stars, bleaching lines and shadows
so they all look happy
and young.

       In the whitening
Adirondack chairs lined up for the photograph,
Gram and the aunts sit next to mom who leans
against an elm and raises a hand
to shield her eyes. William,

the youngest, who lied and enlisted
at 16, will break first
while Jack, his brother
the business wizard, reels between dream
deals, then plummets, senseless,
until they shock him back.

       Halfway through
the next decade, Ray will gas himself
in the womb of his car, the dense expectancy
of Bruckner on the workbench radio, the garage
huge with music.

Dad and Rob will go more slowly,
shot after shot, endless
hours in dark bars, not even love
will bring them home.

        In the corner of the picture
the screened porch next door
is hung with stars, one each
for the dead sons who lived there.
The faces—their mother's, their sisters'—
come back to me in faces of women
whose blood I share. Even now
we map our love with loss.

# I Mean with the Outside Beyond the Walls

Nazim Hikmet
*On Living*

Yesterday I took the train to Brooklyn and at Nevins
I heard the conductor say *This is Heaven.* Then today
you wake up in the Bronx, in Calvary, and the first thing
you see on the wall across from your bed
is a crucifix.

New tumors spring up overnight

like mushrooms after a rain, but the tumors
are hard under your skin under my fingers, ridged
like a bony furbelow, or that portrait of Harta
by Oskar Kokoschka, where one shoulder is really
a stiff black wave that stands out
from the blue aura behind it. It's dusk

in the room and you say, "How did I get here?"
"How did we all get here?" and we don't know
if you mean you, a Jew; all of us nonbelievers
here in a Catholic hospital. Or if only

Monday, in another hospital, another room,
you played the Bach Chaconne—so strong
the man pushing his I.V. down the fluorescent
corridor could remember his body
in the first measured moments
of sex, when it begins like a dance: hands
on her back, fingers touching
each vertebra under her skin, under
her silk blouse. His breath

in small gusts of quarter notes. I can see them
fly from his throat like tiny blackbirds.

I've been trying to remember the 23rd psalm
which for years I said in my head, under my breath,
aloud, in rooms alone, when I was robbed
at gunpoint. Now I need a Bible
in my hands. And it's not enough
not enough. *I am poured out like water;*
*all my bones are out of joint; my heart*
*within my breast is melting wax*

How did I get here?
How did we all get here?

*This is a great adventure, isn't it?*
you say with a dream smile, about to fall asleep.
And I want to order everyone
out of the room, shake you awake—
No! Istanbul! The night all of us, late
again after a concert, ranged
the road to stop a Dolmus for the ferry,
the black lap of the Bosphorus all the way
to Küçüksu. Torches, lanterns and candles,
the palace a lit yalt we could see through
to boats adrift on the river.

*Faaabulous* you say, your famously long "a"
drawn back like that curtain in the shadow
theatre: Karagöz wrestling the demons
of the Underworld. The puppeteer moving figures
in front of a backlit fabric. *Faaabulous*

Jasmine and Magnolia, the Balkin Pine,
the moon like a Byzantine halo.

I could touch your lips and run my fingers
over your throat to remind you
of the wine and Raki.

How did I get here?
How did we all get here?

                    Outside the window

beyond branches that dangle
someone's old sneakers, the Bronx moon
hangs low and gold in the industrial sky. I want to take you there.
Say yes. Say yes.

# The Cardinal

throws its tiny body
at the bedroom window, bone,

feather, flesh, my heart
wild in dream, thumping

like something bludgeoned.
I need to rescue the bird

outside from inside. Arms
holding me back, back,

thick voices warning
danger, but I would kill

to save it. Am I the only one
left in the room growing

brighter and brighter?
Poor bird, poor bird;

it's stunned itself senseless
against the reflection

of mirrored sky.
I'm the one. I'm the one

who labored for hours
on the windows. Vinegar,

newspaper, the old ways
I learned at home

to make glass disappear.

# Elegy for a Drummer

Past midnight, a weeknight, I'm still
sitting in a carved out, windowless place
off Eighth Avenue. The heat

outside's a piston
insisting itself into the dead
center of August. Nobody

smokes anymore. So I just drink
and listen to a trio move through
its predictable paces, waiting

for something to happen.
And then it does—the startlingly
beautiful stolen vernacular

of early Coltrane: *Everytime*
*We Say Goodbye*. It doesn't matter
how many years, I'm back—

record on the stereo, empty
bed tracked with makeup
and sweatsalt. Trane

playing in sheets of music
as though single notes
don't exist. The perfect grief

of the sax, and you—
twenty below, four in the morning
high again, coatless—you call

from the booth on the corner—
*Baby please*—and I'm that woman
in the Czech photograph

Billy sent you from Prague,
the one who stands at a lit window
looking down at a street

so silent she hears
the crash of the milk
before it tilts off the sill.

Your car runs at the curb—exhaust
a white shot of longing
or dread. Snow falls

fine, like dope. You need me
to hold you down making love.
Unanchored you become only part

of the darkness. Breath and smoke
from your cigarette cloud the glass
until your bare hand sweeps

the blurred world into a moment
of focus. My face over yours
a lit whisper, *Witness me.*

Once you told me
*There's no going back.*
*You can't fix things*

*in music, you jump into time*
*then it's over.*
I've imagined that

stillness, the half-cold
air of spring. The road endlessly
unspooling against

a gray blur of morning. Even now,
tonight, in this bar,
in the mix of bourbon and perfume,

in the collective, cooled-off sweat
of strangers, tensed against the inevitable
*Last Call, Last Call ...*

I smell the pungent crush
of new grass as your car bears
the sycamore to rest

at its heart. Blossoms burst, leaves
explode, the gone world falls
around you. *Blue Train* still

playing on tape.

# Gift

Caught here, I love
to think of you moving
your fingers like a blind man
over pearl, ivory, eggshell
papers in this blank book
I'm sending you. I know you
don't record your thoughts,
or sketch, set down ideas
in consonants and vowels,
black and white,
but as I slide my tongue
over the flap of the envelope,
I picture the star sapphire
from your grandfather, glinting, solitary
and splendid on your finger
as your hands move over the pages
I think of as my body.

# My Lost Coat

The black suede trench
I saved up for—
the store beyond my reach—

first time out, flying east
to west to meet you that secret
winter, I left it on the plane.
I must have known

I wouldn't need it there, sand
so hot we raced to water,

as though to burn, I would leave—
everything behind me, the coat, the dark
shape of my life.

# I Imagine I Answer Your Letter

God knows how many blueberries
I've picked since noon—fingers,
lips, tongue, stained
the same blue summer dark
the sky is turning, and I am standing
breathless on a hill on fire
with hawkweed, the sun
dropping into the open mouth
of ocean. If you were here now, you'd know
I'm the same: Never enough
of anything. Remember

the pine-plank table
I built from that old collapse
of barn? Three days into August
it's lined with jars of blue, preserved
and labeled with my name.
Tonight again I'll cook and stir,
drink wine until my legs begin to sway
like reeds, until the sun
takes back the room,
touches every object—the way
blueberries are touched, outside, on the hill.
If you were here now
you'd know I'm the same
woman you left
standing here,
gasping.

V

LISTEN

# Holding On

Last night I dreamed she died in her sleep—
    or was it I
        who died?     And afterward

was it my daughter's voice
           filling the bright
    dream room? Or was *I* speaking


about *my* mother?     She's had everything
    wrong, forever, but never
         her heart

until now in old age. After the first attack

                she calls
from the hospital at dawn

*Oh please come We need*
*to do my hair and makeup*


I went into labor before I knew
         the cord had wound
    itself around my daughter's neck


before I knew
    I would have a heart attack
       giving birth.    So I took my time

and made myself up,

layers of waterproof mascara.

When I cried—bearing down, pushing out
    the next life

                    I wanted to look like myself.

# My Mother's Cars

were almost always red,
the color of Lauren Bacall's lipstick
in *Written on the Wind.*
The years they weren't
they were white, with fins.
One winter when she was driving
a white car, it disappeared
in a Minnesota blizzard
and a semi hit her from behind.
That was the first time
her back was broken. The next,
the dog rushed in the back door
to get out of the cold and pushed her
down the basement stairs. Oh,
the cold. Her cars. Her notoriously
bad driving.
My cousin Tommy rode
a hundred miles on the floor
because he was too terrified to chance
a look out the window. Even my husband
my new, second, husband,
whose calm, judicious nature
my mother and I both loved,
threatened to jump out the door
on her high speed town tour.
*The new city hall! The municipal pool!*
My mother applying lipstick
in the rearview! I was never afraid
with my mother. When she was old
we'd go for the afternoon drives
she loved, and she would get lost
in the town she lived in her whole life.
She'd turn down all the wrong streets
looking, say, for the house

her Dad rented when she was ten—
the one with viburnum and a hundred
and three wooden steps
up the Mississippi bluffs.
And though I knew she was going
in the wrong direction, sometimes
even doubling back, I always believed
she would find it; that there was a secret
way to get there she'd been saving
to show me all my life.

# Before My Mother's Wake

there isn't enough time
to sort the photos, so she's twenty

then holds a grandson. One moment
her mother cradles her

on a spindled porch in Iowa, the next
she's in my father's arms

in a dark ballroom. He's
in black tie, his black hair

smooth as the stone
dropping through nights

she whispers to me
*If only you could have known him before.*

Nearly everything I know
about forgiveness and salvation

is from the dance
that was their marriage—

How she never stopped
reaching for the words

under his image
in the school annual:

*a gentleman from sole to crown.*
How his rage,

—the sway of it—collapsed decades
before he finally stopped,

exhausted by his need for her
to follow.

# How Near, How Far

Remember the day you called to say *Mom,*
*we've got to go hear Les Paul*—pronounced it
*les* like in *Miserables? Eighty-six and still playing*
*at Iridium!* All those years we listened, both of us
so young—"How High the Moon." I guess I never told you
his name. One more thing you were left to puzzle out
on your own. You, the boy with the gaze,
*the eyes that miss nothing* your teacher said.
We were thrilled to get that album for nothing
in one of those Sunday fleas we rooted through
to make a life. Do you remember how
we danced to it? When I stumble
now across photographs you've taken—
the gloss of the page throwing me off
for a moment—and see your images, the mother
I had no way to be then, hears your voice—
distinct, and singular. *This is my world.*
*This is the way I see it.*

# Newfoundland

In my mind's eye he keeps
turning on a dime

to the door he'll forget to lock, keeps
forgetting his coat, this boy

who's just become fatherless, this boy
who's a man, who's our child,

who's on a plane to you now. In his mind
he keeps turning the pages,

of your old text: *Celestial Navigation*
gold sextant embossed on its cover—

horizon mirror, telescope,
graduated arc—

how to move through space
without dead reckoning, measure

the distance between a body
in the heavens and the visible horizon—

the plane dipping, the window giving on snow
on black spruce and white spruce,

balsam, birch—he flies
to the eastern end

of the peninsula Avalon
on the island Newfoundland

to your body.

# Still the Earth

What I remember most
isn't the exhibition, ancient Egyptian
jewelry—faience and silver scarabs, though
you kissed me. Not the Temple
of Dendur, or Cleopatra's Needle
where I told you I have never loved
anyone else. But the shop
where you opened a book on Tuscany
to a double, glossed page of tiled roof,
and tracing one tile with your thumb,
explained the difference between
the Italian and American; why you love
the Italian—that small hatched hinge
between the pieces. The clay unglazed.

# Still

Somewhere up in the Bronx
in rented space I've never seen, seven
rooms of the old life, waiting
in storage. Shrouded wing chairs,
Persian rugs, your mother's
engraved silver, nesting and spooning
in a mahogany box. Racks
of your oils. The body of the grand piano
had to be separated from its legs
so everything could fit—

    I miss our music.

Sunday, on the little radio
I heard Lotte Lenya sing
that song about searching, her urgency
tilted the room, I was that
off balance

and dying to hear it again,
even in my own voice. The ether
offers up dozens of versions, none
the one I wanted. One night,

years into your illness—I was whirling—
singing "Pirate Jenny"
when you calmed me—*Wait*
*sweetheart*, you said, *Lenya*
*is perfectly still*
*when she sings that*
*in the movie.*

It's true. This morning, the light
a slit in the blind, I finally found it
on YouTube. Her body
never moves, only her eyes
and even they stop
near the end. Rapt
I watched it for hours—

Typed your ghost email,
Pressed *send.*

# Listen

What I didn't expect was the cold
the first and last summer
we lived in Paris. The apartment in the eighth
you thought might be too grand was pure
opera—its tiny rooms, the fireplaces
needing fuel all June and July.
And how could I have expected you to move
through that summer on your own two feet?
Once, I read that longing, as a sickness of the heart
is endless, incurable. In my story
you will always walk, you will always
play quartets, you will never be sick
and you will never really die.
                                    How did I manage
in my bad French, to rent a wheelchair?
When you had heartburn from all the pills you took
I asked the pharmacy to send us something
for a "fire in the heart."

Whatever the French celebrated that frozen summer,
it didn't matter, I was there layered
in unserious sweaters. On Bastille Day for the fireworks
at Trocadero, I wore three pairs of cotton socks and scarves
pulled around my neck, my breath in front of me.
I was wild to dance
at each Bastille Ball, in every firehouse,
in every quarter, stunned by wine,
no mind, no body.

Sometimes I used to think of us
as the two parts of that huge stone sculpture
out in front of St-Eustache: You, the poised
recumbent head, and me, the enormous hand,
a finger reaching for the sleeping cheek, longing

to stroke the body back ... *l'Ecoute*
it was called, the whorled ear
big enough for crawling into, cocked

to hear the whole world turning.

# Notes and Dedications

"The Same Hour Has Come Inside My Body" is for my husband, Lorin Bernsohn, in memory. Its title is from the last two lines of section VIII in the poem "Songs" by Antonio Machado. The translation is by Robert Bly.

"From a High Place" takes its title from the book *From a High Place: A Life of Arshile Gorky* by Matthew Spender.

Lac Qui Parle is a French translation of the name given by the Dakota Indians who called it "the lake that speaks."

"Skaters" is for my sisters, Marcia Jarvis, Marjorie Jarvis Miesner, and Mary Jarvis Pribnow.

Itasca is a glacial lake in Northern Minnesota and is the source of the Mississippi River.

"Dakota" is in memory of my grandfather, Frank Jarvis.

"Newfoundland" is for Captain R. James Thorpe, Master Mariner, 1940-2009.

# Acknowledgments

With gratitude to the editors and publishers of the following publications in which versions of these poems first appeared:

*Bellevue Literary Revue*: "I Imagine I Answer Your Letter" and "Holding On"

*Chelsea*: "At the Diebenkorn Show Without You," "I Mean with the Outside Beyond the Walls" and "Sky, River"

*Cream City Review*: "My Father's Songs"

*Gulf Coast*: "Ice Fishing, Lac Qui Parle"

*Mudfish*: "Elegy for a Drummer"

*New Ohio Review*: "Still"

*Notre Dame Review*: "The Same Hour Has Come Inside My Body"

*Poet Lore*: "When I Think of My Mother Laughing"

*Potomac Review*: "Each of Us Diving"

*Seattle Review*: "Where Is North"

*Southern Poetry Review*: "Daylight Savings" and "Listen"

*upstreet*: "Ask Me, 1, 2," "From a High Place" and "My Mother's Cars"

"Listen" was reprinted in *Southern Poetry Review*, 46:2, 2009, and in *Paris, Etc.: Writing and Illustrations* (Copenhagen, Denmark and Florham Park, NJ; Serving House Books, 2016).

"My Mother's Cars" was reprinted in *Best Indie Lit New England*, Vol. 2, 2012-2014.

"The Same Hour Has Come Inside My Body" was reprinted in *Notre Dame Review: The First Ten Years*, 2009.

"Elegy for a Drummer" received the Mudfish Poetry Prize.

"Listen" received the Guy Owen Prize from *Southern Poetry Review*.

"The Same Hour Has Come Inside My Body" received the Lyric Poetry Prize from The Poetry Society of America.

The opening epigraph is from "Slowly— —" in *North in the World: Selected Poems of Rolf Jacobsen* / A Bilingual Edition, Translated, edited, and introduced by Roger Greenwald (The University of Chicago Press, 2002). I am grateful to Roger Greenwald for his translation and for his permission to quote from it.

To Rodger Moody, who made this book possible, thank you for believing in it.

To The MacDowell Colony, my great thanks for the gift of time and space.

I am deeply grateful to Donna Masini who showed me the way.

For their encouragement when it made all the difference, my thanks to Dennis Nurkse and to Vijay Seshadri.

To my first readers, the Riverside Poets, Judy Katz, June Stein, Sally Bliumis-Dunn, and Theresa Burns, my debt is forever. My gratitude for their constancy, insight, wise counsel; their generous spirits and their open hearts.

And special thanks to Frances Richey, who brought order to disorder, and always kept the faith.

For their unfailing and invaluable support and help, and for their friendship, I am enormously grateful to Edward Ballen, Elizabeth Gold, Jessica Greenbaum, M.A. Rocks, and my daughters-in-law, Melineh Kurdian and Nancy Rawlinson. Thank you.

With the deepest possible gratitude to my children, Lucas Thorpe and Amanda Bernsohn, whose love and support sustain me, and whose art inspires me.

And in loving memory of my parents, Luella Foster Jarvis and Alvin E. Jarvis.

# About the Author

Alison Jarvis was born in Canada and grew up in Minnesota. She is a recipient of the Lyric Poetry Prize from the Poetry Society of America, the Mudfish Poetry Prize, the Guy Owen Prize from *Southern Poetry Review*, and a Fellowship from the MacDowell Colony. Her work has appeared in *Cream City Review, Gulf Coast, New Ohio Review, Notre Dame Review, Seattle Review, upstreet*, and other journals and anthologies, including *Best Indie Lit New England*. She lives in Brooklyn, New York, and has been a practicing psychotherapist for 30 years.

# About the Cover Artist

A professional musician and artist, Lorin Bernsohn was born, raised, and lived in New York City his entire life. He began playing the cello as a young child and at 19 after graduating from Manhattan School of Music he joined the Buffalo Philharmonic. He went on to form a number of chamber ensembles which toured widely and in which he made his New York debut. He joined the New York Philharmonic in 1958 where in addition to his orchestral work, he was a member of many Philharmonic chamber groups. From a very early age, he loved painting and drawing and was offered scholarships in both music and art. Although he chose music, in the middle of his life he returned to painting, studying at The Art Students League of New York, eventually becoming a life member. After group and one-man shows in New York, his two passions united when the Philharmonic mounted a one-man show of his work in the then named Avery Fisher Hall.

The interior text and display type as well as the back cover were set in Adobe Jenson, a faithful electronic version of the 1470 roman face of Nicolas Jenson. Jenson was a Frenchman employed as the mintmaster at Tours. Legend has it that he was sent to Mainz in 1458 by Charles VII to learn the new art of printing in the shop of Gutenberg, and import it to France. But he never returned, appearing in Venice in 1468; there his first roman types appeared, in his edition of Eusebius. He moved to Rome at the invitation of Pope Sixtus IV, where he died in 1480.

Type historian Daniel Berkeley Updike praises the Jenson Roman for "its readability, its mellowness of form, and the evenness of color in mass." Updike concludes, "Jenson's roman types have been the accepted models for roman letters ever since he made them, and, repeatedly copied in our own day, have never been equalled."

The display type used on the front cover is Baker Signet, a design on classical lines with subtle but effective calligraphic touches, by Arthur Baker. The author's name was set in Caecilia Italic. This Linotype typeface was designed for his wife, Caecilia. Because its shapes are humanist rather than geometric, PMN Caecilia is easier on the reader's eye and so more useful as a text typeface than most slab serif designs. The award was set in Legato. Designed for legibility, its essential attribute is that the black of the individual letterforms is made equal in importance to the white inside and between the letters. By making the black and white harmonize, Legato approaches an ideal of readability, since reading involves the perception of positive/negative space as one thing. The information detailed at the bottom of the back cover was set in Legato san serif.

Silverfish Review Press is committed to preserving ancient forests and natural resources. We elected to print *Where Is North* on 30% post consumer recycled paper, processed chlorine free. As a result, for this printing, we have saved: 1 tree (40' tall and 6-8" diameter), 499 gallons of water, 293 kilowatt hours of electricity, 64 pounds of solid waste, and 120 pounds of greenhouse gases. Thomson-Shore, Inc. is a member of Green Press Initiative, a nonprofit program dedicated to supporting authors, publishers, and suppliers in their efforts to reduce their use of fiber obtained from endangered forests. For more information, visit www.greenpressinitiative.org.

Cover design by Valerie Brewster, Scribe Typography
Text design by Rodger Moody and Connie Kudura, ProtoType
Printed on acid-free papers and bound by Thomson-Shore, Inc.